# TONY
# BUZA[N]

25 JUN 2013

20. DEC 13.

20. FEB 14,

24. APR 14

21. JUN 14.

# MIND
# MAPPIN[G]

MBS

# TONY BUZAN

# MIND MAPPING

BBC ACTIVE

BBC Active, an imprint of Educational Publishers LLP, part of the Pearson Education Group, Edinburgh Gate, Harlow, Essex, CM20 2JE, England

BBC logo © BBC 1996. BBC and BBC ACTIVE are trademarks of the British Broadcasting Corporation

First published in 2006 by BBC Active
Reprinted 2007

ISBN: 978-0-5635-2034-4

Commissioning Editor: Emma Shackleton
Project Editors: Sarah Sutton and Helena Caldon
Text Designer: Annette Peppis
Cover Designer: R&D & Co Design Ltd
Senior Production Controller: Man Fai Lau
Illustrations by Alan Burton; Mind Map on page 45 is inspired by a Mind Map by Sean Adam

Printed and bound in China CTPSC/02

The Publisher's policy is to use paper manufactured from sustainable forests.

# CONTENTS

# Introduction

The Mind Map® is a dynamic and exciting tool to help all thinking and planning become a smarter and faster activity. The creation of a Mind Map is a revolutionary way to tap into the infinite resources in your brain, to make appropriate decisions, and to understand your feelings.

Those of you who are familiar with my books will know that I first developed the concept of the Mind Map as a learning and memory tool whilst struggling to take effective notes in my student days.

My extraordinary experience and immediate personal success led me to realize that Mind Maps could be developed as a powerful tool for personal transformation and as a way for each of us to make the most of our natural abilities. I had a vision and an ambition that Mind Maps would become a catalyst that would influence a generation of individuals, business thinkers and educators. Over 30 years on, it is an immense source of joy and satisfaction to me that people around the world in all walks of life and at all levels now use Mind Maps as a way of maximizing their individual potential and bringing about personal change.

Mind Maps enable us to plan every aspect of our lives with confidence. They are a tool for communication, problem-solving, creative dreaming, teaching, revising, managing time and recalling memories. They can also be artistic creations in their own right.

For those of you who are new to Mind Maps, this book is the ideal starting point for learning the technique of Mind Mapping, its applications, and the basic principles behind it. It is useful to read it in conjunction with *Buzan Bites: Memory*: firstly so that you will understand more about how the memory functions, and secondly because Mind Maps encapsulate all the creative principles that are necessary to encourage effective recall, and long-term and short-term memory.

For those of you who want to learn still more about this technique, I encourage you to read *The Mind Map® Book*, co-written with my brother, Professor Barry Buzan. It is the definitive guide to creating and using Mind Maps, for life.

I wish you great enjoyment and success as you embark on your Mind Map journey.

Tony Buzan

# A word about terminology

### Key

The Word 'Key' in front of the words 'Word' or 'Image' means much more than 'this is important'. It means this is a 'Memory Key'. The Key Word or Key Image is being developed as a critically important trigger to stimulate your mind, and unlock and retrieve your memories.

### Key Word

A Key Word is a special word that has been chosen or created to become a unique reference point for something important that you wish to remember. Words stimulate the left side of the brain and are a vital component of mastering memory; but they are not as powerful on their own as when you take the time to draw them and transform them into Key Images. When Key Words become Key Images they especially stimulate *both* sides of the brain.

### Key Image

Key Images are the cornerstones of memory and are called *Key Memory Word Images* in my Mind Set books (see Further reading) because they are carefully constructed word-image composites of vital importance in releasing deeply stored memory. A Key Image is much, much more than a picture. It is an image that is linked to and associated with a Key Word. It has been created, using the Memory Principles, to stimulate your imagination and recreate familiar associations. An effective Key Image will stimulate both sides of your brain and draw upon all your senses. Key Images are at the very heart of my Mind Mapping and Memory Techniques.

# 1 WHAT IS A MIND MAP®?

The pages of this bite-sized book will introduce you to one of the most powerful tools for learning and personal discovery that you will ever encounter. Mind Maps are a method of storing, organizing and prioritizing information (usually on paper) using Key Words and Key Images, each of which will trigger specific memories and encourage new thoughts and ideas. Each of the memory triggers in a Mind Map is a key to unlocking facts, ideas and information and, also, to releasing the true potential of your amazing mind so you can become whatever you want to be.

That may sound like an extraordinary claim! The clue to the Mind Map's effectiveness lies in its dynamic shape and form. It is drawn in the shape and form of a brain cell and is designed to encourage your brain to work in a way that is fast, efficient, and in the style that it does naturally.

Every time we look at the veins of a leaf, or the branches of a tree we see nature's 'Mind Maps' echoing the shapes of brain cells and reflecting the way we ourselves are created and connected. Like us, the natural world is forever changing and regenerating, and has a communication structure that appears similar to our own. A Mind Map is a natural thinking tool that draws upon the inspiration and effectiveness of these natural structures.

## Where can you use a Mind Map®?

Mind Maps can be used for any and every purpose in life. The list following includes just a few examples:

⊙ At school: reading, revising, note-taking, developing creative ideas, project management, lecturing.

⊙ At work: brainstorming, time-management, project development, team-building, presentations.

⊙ At home: prioritizing, project-planning, life-planning, shopping, event and household management.

⦿ Socially: keeping track of important dates, remembering people and places, planning holidays and social events, communication.

Mind Maps help us to plan efficiently, manage information effectively, and increase potential for personal success. Those who use Mind Maps as part of daily life, and review personal progress regularly, will usually report that they feel a sense of confidence that their aims are achievable and that they are on track for reaching their goals.

Mind Maps are also useful at times when goals or targets are less clear. Everyone experiences times in life when the future is less than certain. At these times Mind Maps are invaluable for problem-solving. When faced with making difficult decisions, the important thing to remember is that having a goal is always better than having no goal. The benefit of Mind Mapping your vision of the future is that it keeps *you* in the driving seat of your life – and reminds you that you have the freedom to choose your actions and your responses.

A Mind Map can also help you to form more creative ideas and solutions, and to see clearly:
⦿ Where you are: your dreams, your ambitions, your problems and your ideals.
⦿ Who you are: at home, in your work, at leisure and in relationships.
⦿ How you see the world: your relationship with others.
⦿ What you want: for yourself, for others, for today, for the future.
⦿ How to get to where you want to be!

A Mind Map is also invaluable for gathering and ordering information, to identify the Key Words and facts from:

- Books, newspapers, Internet resources
- Lectures, course notes, research material
- Business meetings, minutes, conversations, lists
- Your own head!

Mind Maps are especially useful in schools for and other forms of training and education. More information about practical applications for Mind Maps in these fields can be found in *The Mind Map® Book* (BBC Active) and other titles listed on page 95.

Many of the examples in this book focus on practical decision-making and how Mind Maps can be used as a tool for life. Always be prepared to ask yourself the big questions, such as: 'What would you like history to say about you, or your accomplishments?' Thinking 'big' will focus you on the long term and will sharpen your immediate actions and choices.

In Chapters 4 and 5 we will get down to the business of creating and using Mind Maps; first it is important to understand something about the way the brain works, how we think, and how this leads, naturally, to the Mind Map concept.

# 2 MIND MATTERS

## How your brain works

Your amazing brain began to evolve over 500 million years ago, and yet we have known that it is located in your head, and not your heart, for only 500 years. Even more amazing is the fact that 95 per cent of what we know about the brain and how it works was discovered within the last ten years. We have so much more to learn!

Your brain is an extraordinary, super-powered processor capable of boundless thoughts and Radiant Thinking. It has five major functions:

- ⊙ *Receiving* – The brain receives information via your senses.
- ⊙ *Storing* – It retains and stores the information and is able to access it on demand. (Although it may not always feel that way to you!)
- ⊙ *Analyzing* – Your brain recognizes patterns and likes to organize information in ways that make sense: by examining information and questioning meaning.
- ⊙ *Controlling* – The brain controls the way you manage information in different ways, depending upon your state of health, your personal attitude and your environment.
- ⊙ *Outputting* – The brain outputs received information via our thoughts, speech, through drawing, movement, and all other forms of creativity.

A Mind Map is designed to utilize these abundant brain skills by helping your brain to store and retrieve information effectively and on demand.

## Linear vs. whole brain thinking

For hundreds of years, because we speak and write in sentences, we have assumed that ideas and information should be stored in a linear, or list-like, fashion. This is self-limiting, as we shall see.

In speech we are limited to saying only one word at a time; likewise, in print, words are presented in lines and sentences, with beginnings, middles and ends. This linear emphasis continues in schools, colleges and the workplace, where most people are encouraged to take notes in sentence and bullet-point form.

The limitation of this approach is that it can take quite a while to get to the core issue of the matter, and during this process you will say, hear, or read a great deal that is not essential for long-term recall.

Recent research has shown that the brain is a multi-dimensional faculty that is capable of absorbing, interpreting and recalling information in ways that are far more sensual, creative, multi-faceted and immediate than speech and written words. Your mind is perfectly capable of, and is *designed* for, taking in information that is non-linear, and does so all the time: when looking at photographs, pictures or interpreting the images that are around you every day.

The brain, when listening to a series of spoken sentences, does not absorb information word by word, line by line; it takes in the information as a whole, sorts it, interprets it, and feeds it back to you in a multitude of ways. You hear each word and put it in the context of existing knowledge as well as the other words around it. You do not need to have heard the entire range of sentences before forming a response.

*For example:*
◉ You might telephone a talking timetable to receive information about the 18.50 train home from Waterloo to Exeter. Before the automatic voice has made any mention of Exeter, you are told that there are *delays* at Clapham Junction, the first stop just outside Waterloo station.

⦿ In a split second, your brain will begin to make associations: *feelings* associated with returning home, or sleeping in a comfortable bed; the *sounds* of people's voices and platform announcements; the *smell* and *taste* of a delicious evening meal. All of which leave you weighing up whether to make the journey in your car, travel on a coach, or stay overnight in London instead of getting the 18.50 train.

⦿ The reason for this response is that the word 'delay' has acted as a Key Word that has triggered a multi-faceted response before you have heard one word of specific information relating to your original question, and before the talking timetable has finished its sentence.

⦿ Getting home is still your main aim – but the delay has, for the present time, become the central concept.

Key Words and their context are vitally important memory triggers, and it is the network inside the mind that is of most importance in helping to understand and interpret our world.

## How we waste time making notes

We are so used to speaking and writing words that we have come to believe that normal sentences are the best way to store and recall verbal images and ideas. In fact, over 90 per cent of written notes taken by students are superfluous, because your brain naturally prefers Key Words that represent the big picture. This means that:

⦿ Time is wasted recording words that have no bearing on memory.

⦿ Time is wasted re-reading unnecessary words.

⦿ Time is wasted searching for Key Words that have not been highlighted in any way and therefore blend in with the whole.

⊙ Time is wasted when the connections between Key Words are slowed down by extraneous connecting words.

⊙ Distance weakens associations between Key Words. The further apart they are, the weaker the associations.

Mind Maps are now being used by schools, businesses, government organizations and individuals around the world. This system of note-taking creates a complete, at-a-glance representation of an idea, concept or plan which is presented in a simple fusion of words and pictures.

## Your brain and Mind Maps

Rather than starting at the beginning and continuing stage by stage until you reach the end, a Mind Map starts with the central concept and radiates outwards to take in the detail. A Mind Map has a number of advantages over standard note-taking:

⊙ The central idea is more clearly defined.

⊙ The relative importance of each idea is clearly identified.

⊙ The more important ideas are immediately recognizable at the centre of the Mind Map.

⊙ The links between key concepts are immediately identifiable, encouraging association of ideas and concepts.

⊙ Review of information is effective and rapid.

⊙ The structure of a Mind Map allows additional concepts to be added easily.

⊙ Each Mind Map is a unique creation – which will in turn aid accurate recall.

In Chapters 4 and 5, I will explain how to create Mind Maps, how they can be used and for what purposes; first I want to introduce you to the concept of 'Radiant Thinking'. Radiant

Thinking® describes the way the brain creates thoughts and ideas. A Mind Map also mirrors the activity of the brain by being organized in a Radiant way, thereby triggering creative thoughts and memories more effectively.

# 3 RADIANT THINKING®

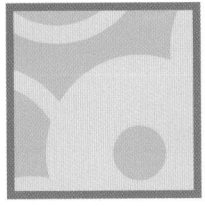

To understand why Mind Maps are so effective, it is helpful to know more about the way your brain thinks and remembers information. Your brain does not think in a linear, monotonous way, rather it thinks in multiple directions simultaneously – starting from central trigger points in Images or Key Words. I describe this as *Radiant Thinking*.

As the term suggests, thoughts radiate outwards like the branches of a tree, the veins of a leaf or the blood vessels of the body that emanate from the heart.

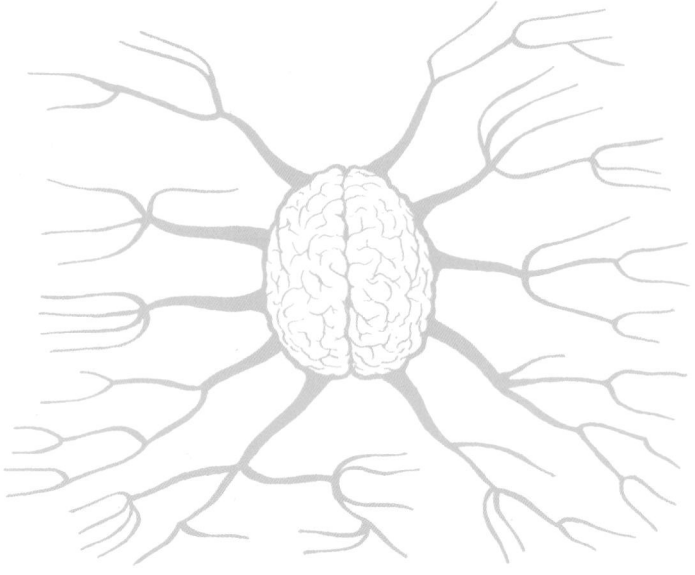

Your brain has the ability to create an infinite number of ideas, visions and concepts. A Mind Map is designed to work in the same way as your brain, and is a reflection on paper of Radiant Thinking in action. The more closely you can record information in a way that reflects the natural workings of your brain, the more efficiently your brain will be able to trigger the recall of essential facts and personal memories.

# Radiant Thinking® exercise

To show you what I mean, try the following exercise, which will demonstrate the extraordinary power of your Radiant Thinking mind. I am going to ask you to conjure up an image that you will have no time to think about in advance, but I guarantee that you will get the answer right.

The word I would like you to consider is:

### BANANA

You did not hear me say the word, but nevertheless:
- Did you see an *image*?
- Was there *colour* in the image?
- How *quickly* did you get the image?
- *What* was the image?
- *What* were the associations around the image?
- *Where* was it before it appeared?!

Most people around the world are familiar with what a banana looks like. When you 'heard' the word you may have seen the *colours* yellow, brown, or green - depending on the ripeness of the fruit. You may have seen its curved *shape*. You may have associated the image with a delicious dessert, an exotic holiday or a fruity drink. The image will have appeared instantaneously, as if from nowhere, and you are unlikely to have spent any time visualizing the letters of the word. The image was already stored in your mind; you simply needed to trigger its release.

This quick test shows that everyone, whatever their sex, status or nationality, uses Radiant Thinking to link Key Word associations with Key Images – instantaneously. This is the basis for *all* our thinking; and this is the basis of Mind Maps.

**Mind Maps have been devised to enhance and increase the Radiant Thinking process.**

## How Key Words and Key Images work

A Key Word, or phrase, is one that represents a specific image or range of images.

A Key Image is one which, when transmitted to your brain, will enable you to recall not just the single word or phrase, but a whole wealth of related information in multi-dimensional form.

*For example:*

◉ When trying to find an image to encapsulate the concept of going to a funfair as a child, you might choose the word 'candyfloss'.

◉ The word 'candyfloss' will, as a Key Word, trigger your analytical left-brain memory.

◉ Drawing a picture of candyfloss will create a Key Image, which will engage your visual right-brain memory.

◉ The picture will become a visual trigger that will represent not only the written word, but also the sights, smells, sounds and taste of the funfair.

The word on its own is not enough to trigger the entire experience of the funfair, because it is not engaging your whole brain. The word as part of a sentence will not trigger the entire experience either, because a sentence defines and limits. The purpose of a Key Word that has been transformed into a drawn Key Image, on the other hand, is to connect with both the left-brain and the right-brain functions. This action will radiate connections and trigger recall of complete associated information.

# The language of the brain

The main language of your brain is neither the spoken nor the written word. Your brain works via your senses by creating associations between images, colours, key words and ideas.

Long before human beings knew what the brain was or where it was, the ancient Greeks discovered that to be able to recall information on demand and to trigger memory accurately, they needed to use a combination of:

## Imagination and Association

Imagination and association are connected to whole brain activity. Your imagination is stimulated mainly when you use:

- Your senses
- Exaggeration
- Rhythm and movement
- Colour
- Laughter
- Pictures and images.

Association is stimulated mainly when you use:

- Numbers
- Words
- Symbols
- Order
- Patterns
- Images.

We are all attracted to people who make us feel good and things that we enjoy. In order for your Mind Map to become something that you enjoy looking at, and want to keep referring to, it needs to be:

⊙ *a positive representation* of events or plans; and
⊙ *attractive* to look at.

A Mind Map that includes these important factors will encourage your brain to associate, link and connect your thoughts, fears, dreams and ideals in ways that are far more creative than any other form of note-taking. A Mind Map triggers associations in your brain that will help you to come up with ideas, reach conclusions, and make plans more quickly and creatively than any other form of brainstorming technique.

## Radiant Thinking and Key Word exercise

The mini Mind Map below is going to represent the concept of 'happiness'. There is space around the word for ten Key Word associations.

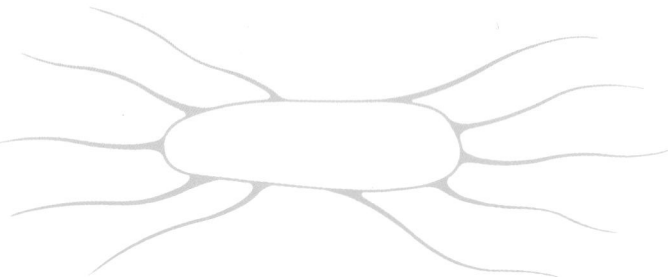

Try completing this exercise either on your own, or with two or three other people. (It is important not to discuss your associations, as by doing so you will influence each other.)
⊙ First draw a central image that represents 'happiness' for you.
⊙ Then, on each of the branches around the edge, write the first ten Key *Word* associations that radiate from the centre when you think of the picture you have drawn to represent 'happiness'.

◉ It is important to put down the first words that come to mind, no matter how ridiculous you may think they are. Don't self-censor or give yourself pause for thought.

◉ If you find it easy to think of more than ten words, include them by drawing extra branches for them.

When you have finished, compare your results with other people's, to see which words overlap.

The point of this exercise is to show that once your brain begins to 'freewheel' in word association, it doesn't slow down. Rather like following links on the Internet, you will find yourself thinking of many more connections.

Another point is that if you compare your results with other people's, you will be surprised at how little overlap there is between the choices of associated words. We really are unique as individuals, and we really do think in a Radiant way!

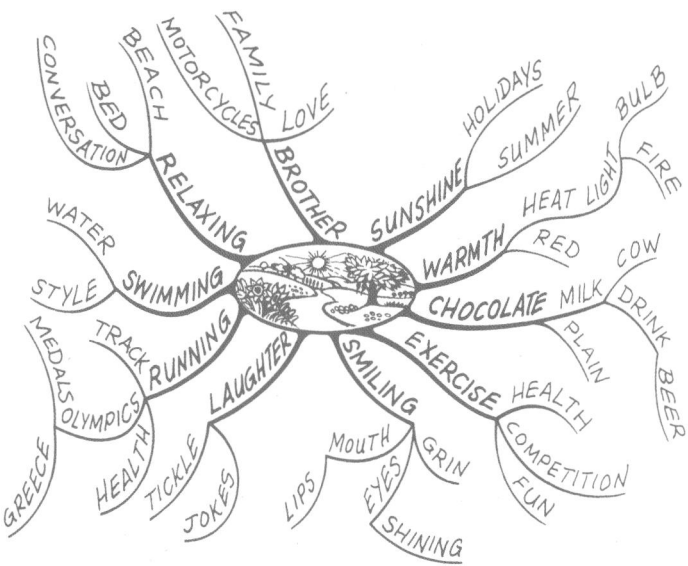

# 4  THE MIND MAP® RULES

This chapter will explain how to prepare to Mind Map: the importance of goal-setting; what needs to be planned in advance; how to order your ideas; and the importance of Key Words and Images. This will prepare you for Chapter 5, which includes step-by-step guidelines on how to create Mind Maps for the major situations and purposes in life.

## Setting your goal

A Mind Map represents a personal thought-journey on paper, and like any successful journey it needs some planning in order to be successful. The first step before starting your Mind Map is to decide where you are headed.

- What is your goal or vision?
- What are the sub-goals and categories that contribute to your goal?
- Are you planning a project?
- Are you brainstorming ideas?
- Do you need to take stock of a current situation?
- Are you making a strategic plan for the future?

Making this decision is important because a successful Mind Map has at its heart a core image which represents your goal, and your first step will be to *draw a picture* in the centre of your Mind Map to represent that goal as a success.

## The power of pictures

The adage that 'a picture is worth a thousand words' is true. In an experiment, scientists showed a group of people 600 images at a rate of one per second. When tested for accurate recall after the presentation, there was a 98 per cent rate of accurate recall across the whole group. The human brain finds it much easier to remember images than words and this is why, in a Mind Map, the central key idea is replaced by an image. Using images elsewhere in your Mind Map is also important.

**Exercise**
To practise your image-association skills, look back at the mini Mind Map you created for the word 'happiness'. See whether you can re-create the whole Mind Map using images only.

As explained on page 25 , we like to be near to people and things that make us feel good; that are positive and attractive. In order to make sure that your Mind Map becomes a genuinely useful tool that you want to develop, the central image on your Mind Map needs to be multi-coloured and designed to appeal all your senses. It does not need to be beautifully drawn or wonderfully artistic, but it does need to make you feel positive and focused when you look at it.

> A Mind Map not only *uses* images, in its entirety it *is* an image – one that represents your vision or goal.

When you create such a positive vision, it will take on a life and energy of its own and will help you to stay focused. When you are focused you become the human equivalent of a very powerful laser beam: precise, goal-directed and phenomenally powerful.

# Gathering and ordering your thoughts

After giving your Radiant Thinking creativity free rein, it is important next to edit and organize your ideas by introducing more structure.

The first step towards adding structure is to decide on your Basic Ordering Ideas (BOIs). BOIs are the underlying key themes around which all other concepts can be organized. They are the 'hooks' on which to hang all associated ideas (just as the chapter headings of a book represent the thematic content within the pages).

*For example:*

The basic concept 'food' has many sub-categories, such as fruit, vegetables and meat. Depending on what your purpose is, you may choose to sub-divide the sub-category 'fruit' into broad categories, such as citrus and non-citrus, before considering the types of fruit and their uses. Alternatively, you may be exploring the concept of 'favourite foods', in which case the categories are unimportant and you may leap from 'fruit' straight to banana, strawberry, papaya, etc.

For your Mind Map of your life plans, useful personal BOI categories could include:

**Personal history: past, present, future**

**Strengths      Weaknesses      Likes      Dislikes**

**Long-term goals      Family      Friends**

**Achievements      Hobbies      Emotions**

**Work      Home      Responsibilities**

Other helpful BOIs may be concerned with the direction your life is taking:

Learning    Knowledge    Business
Health    Travel    Leisure
Culture    Ambitions    Problems

BOIs are the chapter headings of your thoughts: the words or images that represent the simplest and most obvious categories of information. They are the words that will automatically attract your brain to think of the greatest number of associations.

If you are not sure what your BOIs should be, ask yourself the following simple questions with regard to your main goal or vision:

⊙ What knowledge is required to achieve my aim?

⊙ If this were a book, what would the chapter headings be?

⊙ What are my specific objectives?

⊙ What are the seven most important categories in this subject area?

⊙ What are the answers to my basic questions: Why? What? Where? Who? How? Which? When?

⊙ Is there a larger, more encompassing, category that all of these fit into that would be more appropriate to use?

The advantages of having well-thought-out BOIs are:

⊙ The primary ideas are in place, so the secondary ideas will follow more naturally.

⊙ The BOIs help to shape, sculpt and construct the Mind Map which encourages your mind to think in a naturally structured way.

When you decide upon your first set of Basic Ordering Ideas before you begin Mind Mapping, the rest of your ideas will flow in a far more coherent and useful way.

## Getting started

To create effective Mind Maps you will need a stock of
paper, some multi-coloured pens, at least 10–20 minutes of
uninterrupted time – and your brain!

◉ Make sure you have a blank exercise book filled with plain
pages, or a quantity of good-quality, LARGE-sized sheets of
BLANK, unlined paper.

◉ You will need a range of MULTI-COLOURED pens in fine,
medium and highlighter thickness that flow easily and with
which you can write comfortably and quickly.

### Why?

◉ You need PLENTY of paper, because this is not just a
practical exercise, it is a personal journey. You will want to refer
back to your Mind Maps over time to assess your progress and to
review your goals.

◉ You need LARGE-sized sheets of paper because you will want
space to explore your ideas. Small pages will cramp your style.

◉ The pages should be BLANK and UNLINED in order to free
your brain to think in a non-linear uninhibited and creative way.

◉ An exercise book or ring binder of paper is best because your
first Mind Map is the start of a working journal. You don't want
to be subconsciously inhibited by a need to be 'neat', and you
will want to keep all your ideas together in order to see how your
plans and needs evolve over time.

◉ You need easy-flowing pens because you will want to be able
to read what you have created and may want to write fast.

◉ A selection of colours is important because colour stimulates
your brain and will activate creativity and visual memory.

◉ Colour also allows you to introduce structure, weight and
emphasis to your Mind Map.

# Mind Maps: the guiding principles

The Mind Map laws are divided into:

⊙ Technique
⊙ Layout.

The laws of technique are:

⊙ Use emphasis
⊙ Use association
⊙ Be clear
⊙ Develop a personal style.

The laws of layout are:

⊙ Use hierarchy
⊙ Use numerical order.

## Summary of the Mind Map Laws

### Techniques

**1    Emphasis**

Always use:

⊙ A central image – to provide a focus.
⊙ Images – to coordinate both sides of your brain.
⊙ Three or more colours per central image – to stimulate memory and creativity.
⊙ Dimension in images and around words – to make things stand out.
⊙ A blend of your physical senses: sight, sound, taste, touch, smell, spatial awareness – to make it real and memorable.
⊙ Variations of size of letters, lines and images – to

distinguish levels of importance.

⊙ Organized spacing – to keep the line rules ordered, appealing, and to allow room for additions.

⊙ Appropriate spacing – around each word or image.

## 2 Association

Always use:

⊙ Arrows – to guide the eye when you want to make connections.

⊙ Colours – to improve your memory, enhance creativity and increase recall.

⊙ Codes – such as ticks, crosses, triangles, under-linings as short-cuts, which can be used to create associations across the Mind Map.

## 3 Be clear

⊙ Use only one Key Word per line.

⊙ Print all words.

⊙ Print Key Words on lines.

⊙ Make line length equal to word length.

⊙ Make major branches connect to central image.

⊙ Connect lines to other lines.

⊙ Make central lines thicker.

⊙ Make your images clear.

⊙ Keep your page horizontal.

⊙ Keep your printing upright.

## 4 Develop a personal style

You will relate to, and remember more easily, something that you have created yourself.

## Techniques
### 1   Emphasis

Emphasis is one of the most important factors in improving memory and creativity. For more explanation as to why this is so, please refer to *Buzan Bites: Memory*, which describes why we remember images, words, people or events that stand out more easily than those that are routine or that blend in.

**Always use a central image**

⊙ An image automatically focuses your eye and your brain. It triggers numerous associations and is a highly effective memory aid.

⊙ In addition, an image that is appealing will please you and draw attention to itself.

⊙ If a word, rather than a picture, is used as the central image, it can be made more three-dimensional by the addition of shade, colour or attractive lettering.

**Use images throughout your Mind Map**

⊙ Using images throughout your Mind Map will add more focus and make your Mind Map more attractive. It will also help you to 'open your mind' to the world around you, and will stimulate both the left-brain and the right-brain in the process.

◉ Use three or more colours per central image. Colours stimulate memory and creativity: they wake up the brain. This is in contrast to monochrome (one colour) images, which the brain sees as monotonous: they send the brain to sleep!

◉ Use dimension both in images and around words; this will help things to stand out, and whatever stands out is more easily remembered. Using dimension is especially effective in giving Key Words prominence.

### Use your senses

◉ Your brain receives messages via your senses: sight, hearing, touch, taste and spatial awareness. Many of the world's great minds have consciously used and developed all their senses in order to learn more about the world around them. The more your Mind Map can evoke sensual memory, the more powerful it will be.

### Use variations of printing, line and image

◉ Varying the size of the type on your Mind Map will introduce a sense of hierarchy and give a clear message regarding the relative importance of the items listed.

### Use organized spacing

◉ Organizing the look of the branches of the Mind Map on the page will help communicate the hierarchy and categorization

of ideas, and will also make
it easier to read and more
attractive to look at.

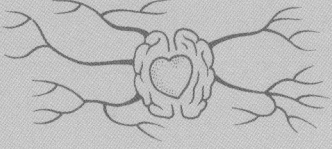

## Use appropriate spacing

◉ It is important to leave the right amount of space around
each item on your Mind Map, partly so that each item can be
seen clearly, and partly because space itself is an important part
of communicating a message.

## 2  Association

Association is the second major factor necessary for improving
memory and creativity. The brain creates association between
events and things by joining them together with linking
information. Association is the means by which your brain
makes sense of your physical experience of life.

The following techniques are methods for creating
association between different themes, ideas and events on your
Mind Map.

## Use arrows when you want to make connections
## within and across the branches

◉ Arrows guide your eye in a way that will automatically join
things together. Arrows also suggest movement. Movement is a
valuable aid to effective memory and recall.

◉ Arrows can point in one direction, or in several directions at
once, and they can be of all shapes and sizes.

## Use colours

⊙ Colour is one of the most powerful tools for enhancing memory and creativity.

⊙ Choosing specific colours for coding purposes will give you faster access to the information contained in your Mind Map and will help you to remember it more easily.

⊙ Colour-coding is especially useful in group Mind Map situations.

## Use codes

⊙ Codes save a lot of time. They enable you to make instant connections between different parts of your Mind Map, however far apart they may be on the page.

⊙ Codes may take the form of ticks, crosses, circles, triangles, underlining, or they can be more elaborate.

## 3 Be clear

The clearer you can be, the more you and others will understand. Scribbled notes obscure memory and understanding and inhibit your brain's ability to make associations.

## Use only one Key Word per line

⊙ Each individual word will conjure up many thousands of possible connotations and associations.

⊙ By placing one word per line, you have maximum opportunity to make associations for each word. In addition every word is connected to the word or image that sits alongside it on the next line. In this way, your brain is opened up to new thoughts.

### Print all words
⊙ Printed words are more defined in shape and are therefore easier for your mind to 'photograph' and retain.

⊙ The extra time it takes to print a word is more than made up for by the advantages it creates of increased speed of association and recall.

⊙ Printing also encourages brevity, and can be used to emphasize the relative importance of words.

### Print Key Words on lines
⊙ The lines on a Mind Map are important as they connect the individual Key Words together.

⊙ Your Key Words need to be connected to the lines to help your brain make the connection with the rest of your Mind Map.

### Make line length equal to word length
⊙ If words and their lines are of equal length they will look more effective and will connect more easily to the words on either side of them.

⊙ The space saved will allow you to add more information to your Mind Map.

### Connect lines to other lines and major branches to the central image
⊙ Connecting the lines on your Mind Map will help you to connect the thoughts in your mind.

⊙ Lines can be transformed into arrows, curves, loops, circles, ovals, triangles or any other shape you choose.

## Make the central lines thicker and keep them curved

⊙ Thicker lines will send the message to your brain that they are the most important, so thicken up all central lines. If, to begin with, you are uncertain which ideas are going to be the most important, you can thicken the lines once you have finished.

## Create shapes and boundaries around your Mind Map branches

⊙ Shapes encourage your imagination.

⊙ Creating shapes in your Mind Map – for example by creating a shape around a branch of a Mind Map – will help you to remember the many themes and ideas more easily.

## Make your images as clear as possible

⊙ Clarity on the page encourages clarity of thought. A clear Mind Map will also be more elegant, graceful and pleasant to use.

## Keep the paper arranged horizontally in front of you

⊙ The 'landscape' format of the page will give you optimum freedom to draw and create your Mind Map.

⊙ It will also be easier to read once you have finished it.

## Keep printing as upright as possible

⊙ Upright printing gives your brain easier access to the thoughts expressed on the page; this applies to the angle of the lines as well as of the words.

## 4   Develop a personal style

Each one of us is astonishing and unique and our Mind Maps are an opportunity to show that uniqueness and to celebrate your individual thought processes.

Each time you create a Mind Map, make the new one slightly more colourful, more three-dimensional, more imaginative and more beautiful than the last. This will not only make it easier for you to identify with the Mind Map, it will also have the added benefit of constantly developing and refining all your mental skills.

The more personal your Mind Maps are, the easier you will remember them.

## Layout

The way you lay out and structure your Mind Map will have an immense impact on how you use it, and its practical 'usability'.

## 1   Use hierarchy

⊙ As discussed earlier (see page 32), the use of hierarchy and categorization – in the form of Basic Ordering Ideas – will help your brain's power of recall enormously.

## 2   Use numerical order

⊙ If your Mind Map is the basis for an action, such as a project, a speech, or a holiday, you will need to order your thoughts – whether chronologically or in order of importance.
⊙ To do this, simply number the branches in the desired order of action or priority.
⊙ Other levels of detail, such as time or dates, can be added if preferred. Letters of the alphabet could also be used, instead of numbers.

# What to avoid when Mind Mapping

The next chapters will explain how Mind Maps can be created, used and applied in different areas of our life. Before moving on, however, it may be useful to take a look at what happens when a Mind Map does not turn out as planned.

There are four danger areas that face any Mind Mapper:

⊙ The creation of Mind Maps that aren't really Mind Maps.

⊙ Using phrases instead of single words.

⊙ Unnecessary concern about creating a 'messy' Mind Map.

⊙ A negative emotional response to your Mind Map.

## When a Mind Map is not a Mind Map

Take a look at the following cluster shapes. Each of them represents an early Mind Map drawn by someone who hasn't quite grasped the basics.

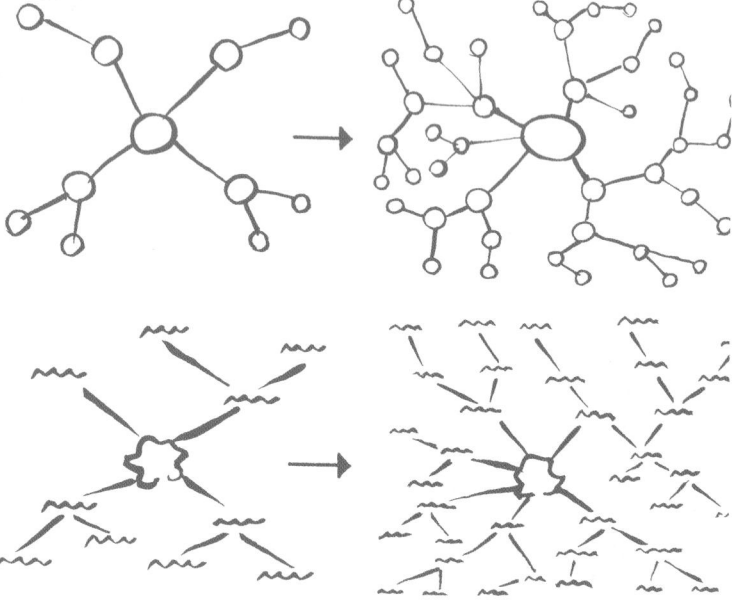

At first glance they may seem acceptable, but in fact they ignore the key principle of 'Radiant Thinking'. Each idea is on its own, cut off from the others. There is no dynamic connection between the branches and nothing to encourage the brain to spark with new ideas. They are designed to cut off thought.

Compare this with the outline of a Mind Map that closely follows all the important principles:

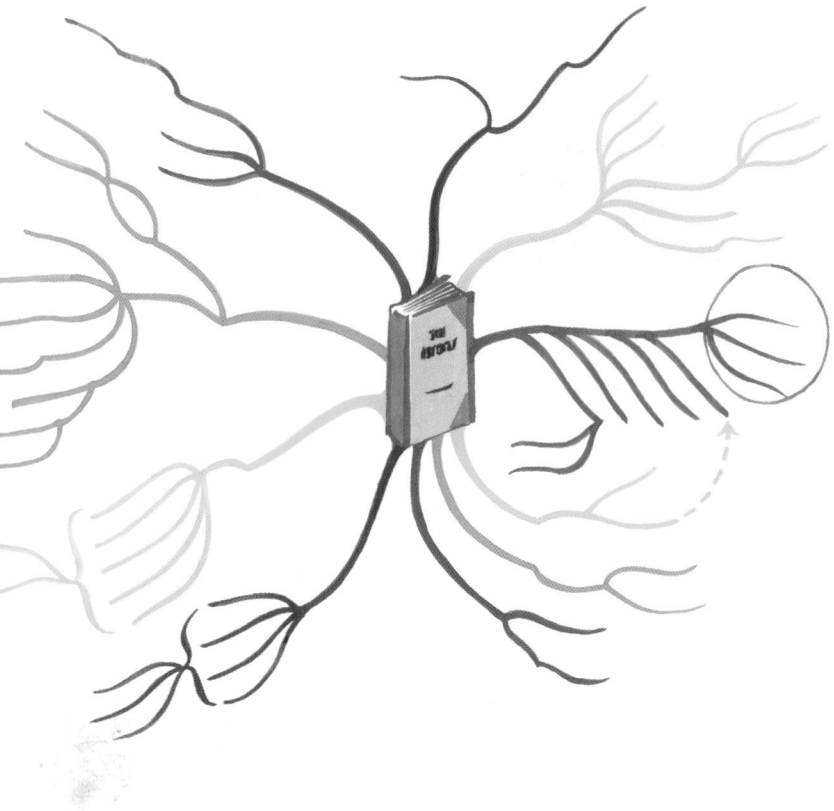

Remember, a *true* Mind Map opens up thought in a Radiant way (see page 27).

## Why words are better than phrases

Take a look at the three images below as they illustrate perfectly
why a phrase does not work well in a Mind Map or good thinking.

⊙ The first version, showing the three words all together on
the same line, is ineffective because there is no escape from the
'unhappiness' of the phrase.

⊙ The second version is an improvement as it has opened the
phrase out into its component parts and therefore enables free
association to take place with each word. However, the words-only
approach means that it is appealing mainly to the left side of the
brain, and is limiting the brain's creative response to the words.
Nor is it completely clear which of the words is the core concept.

⊙ The third version follows all Mind Map rules. It is no longer
a completely negative picture. The cause of the unhappiness can

be seen to be separate from the afternoon itself and the basic concept of happiness has been introduced into the equation. It is a dynamic image where change and choice are possible.

## When a messy Mind Map is a good Mind Map

Depending on your circumstances when note-taking, it may not always be possible to create a neat and tidy Mind Map. If you are in a lecture or a meeting, or in a situation where ideas are not being presented in an ordered fashion, it will not always be possible to identify immediately the core concepts. Your Mind Map will reflect that organic situation and will be an accurate reflection of your state of mind at the time.

However 'messy' the Mind Map is, it is still likely to contain more information of value than would have been the case had you noted everything down. Take some time immediately after such a lecture or meeting to transform your Mind Map notes into a more constructive form. Use:

- Arrows
- Symbols
- Highlighting
- Images.

and other devices, to identify the Basic Ordering Ideas and to instil hierarchy, associations and colour into your notes. If necessary, re-draw your Mind Map following the basic rules, so that the information is made easier for your memory to recall in future.

## **Your personal style**

As well as having a practical purpose, Mind Maps help you to develop your artistic and creative personality. Many of my students and associates over the years have turned the creation of Mind Maps into an art form! (If you look at the colour plates in *The Mind Map® Book* you will see many examples of this.)

A Mind Map harnesses all of your brain's abilities to interpret words, images, numbers, logic, rhythm, colour and spatial awareness, in a single powerful technique. It gives you the freedom to roam wherever your mind takes you.

Creating your own artistic Mind Maps will help to:

⊙ Develop your artistic skills and visual perception, which will in turn enhance your memory, creative thought and your self-confidence.

⊙ Reduce stress, improve relaxation and act as an intriguing form of self-discovery.

The next chapter will look at the creative process in more detail, and will answer any questions you may have about how to Mind Map.

# 5 CREATING A MIND MAP®

The previous chapters have explained the tools, the rules and the common errors of Mind Map creation. This chapter will take a step by step look at how to Mind Map, how to apply Mind Maps, and how to use Mind Maps as a tool for life-planning, making decisions, and for taking action.

## Creating a Mind Map

You have gathered your materials, you have read the guidelines, and now you have a sense of why a Mind Map is more than just a collection of ideas on a page. So it's time to begin:

**1** **Focus** on your central aim, desire or vision. Be clear about what it is that you are aiming for or trying to resolve. (If you need some extra help in deciding what your main priority is, turn to page 32 for guidance.)

**2** Turn your first sheet of paper **sideways** in front of you (landscape-style), in order to start creating your Mind Map in the centre of the page. This will allow you freedom of expression, without being restricted by the narrow measure of the page.

**3** Draw an **image** in the centre of the blank sheet of paper to represent your goal. Don't worry if you feel that you can't draw well; that doesn't matter.

It is very important to use an image as the starting point for your Mind Map because an image will jump-start your thinking by activating your imagination. The more images you use throughout the Mind Map, the more the visual impact on your brain/memory will be reinforced.

**4** From the outset, use **colour** for emphasis, structure, texture, creativity, and to add an element of fun to your thinking. This will stimulate your visual sense and reinforce the image in your mind.

Try to use at least three colours overall, and create your own colour-coding system. Colour can be used hierarchically or thematically, or it can be used to emphasize certain points.

**5** Now draw a series of **thick lines**, radiating out from the centre of the image. These are the primary branches of your Mind Map and will support your idea like the sturdy branches of a tree.

It is important that you **connect** the primary branches firmly to the central image, because the brain, and therefore the memory, operates by association.

**6** Make your lines **curved** rather than straight because they are more interesting to your eye and more memorable to your brain.

**7**  On each branch, write *one* **Key Word** that you associate with the topic. These are your **Main Thoughts** (and your Basic Ordering Ideas), relating to themes such as:

**Situation**      **Feelings**      **Facts**      **Choices**

Remember that using only one Key Word per line allows you to define the very essence of the issue you are exploring, whilst also helping to make the association be stored more emphatically in your brain. Phrases and sentences limit the effect and confuse your memory.

**8**  Add a few **empty branches** to your Mind Map. Your brain will want to put something on them!

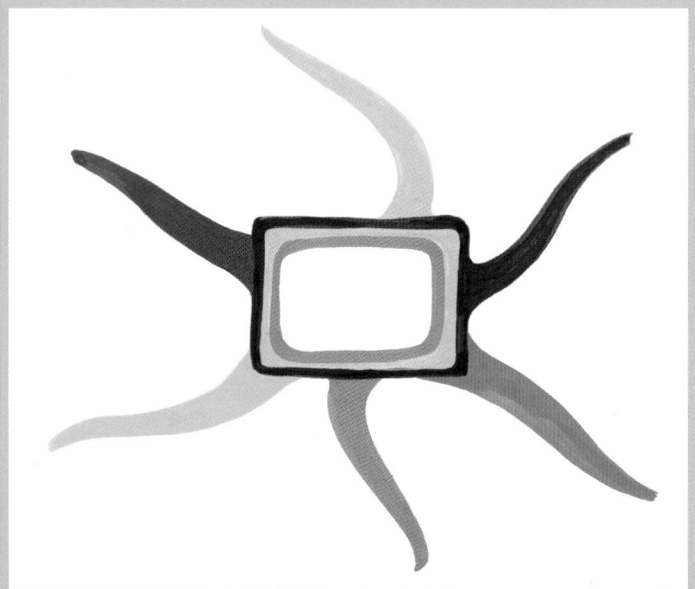

**9** Next, create second- and third-level branches for your related **Associated** and **Secondary Thoughts**. The secondary level connects to the primary branches, the third level to the secondary branches, and so on. Association is everything in this process.

The words that you choose for each of your branches can relate to anything that is concerning you at the moment. You may want to include themes that ask questions: the **Who**, **What**, **Where**, **Why**, **How** of the subject or situation, as well as your **Personal Choices** for action and change.

On pages 54–61 following, the Mind Map process is broken down into fast and easy stages that will help you to practise the technique one step at a time before building the results into a complete Mind Map.

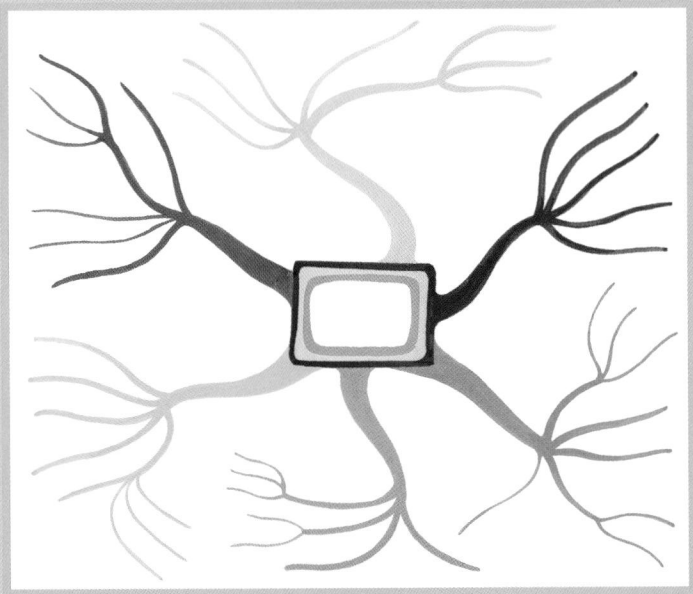

## Ideas into action

Your completed Mind Map is both a picture of your thoughts and the first stage in preparing a plan of action. Prioritizing and weighting your themes and conclusions can be done quite simply by numbering each branch of the Mind Map.

Make your most important point 1, the next most important 2, then 3, 4 and so on. Connecting points can be linked using arrows or colour-coding, as described on pages 36–7.

## Decision-making with Mind Maps

When life-planning or making choices, Mind Maps are ideal because they help you reach a balanced viewpoint of your situation. The next sections take you through the decision-making process step by step.

## Identify facts and feelings

⊙ Do you tend to make decisions or form opinions based on your emotions and instinct – sometimes at the expense of common sense and rationality?

⊙ Do you tend to make decisions based on logical deduction – sometimes at the expense of your own true needs and wants?

⊙ Do you find it hard to take a balanced view of a situation if you have already formed an opinion?

Most people will answer 'yes' to at least one of these questions. A useful way to encourage your brain to be more creative and balanced in approach is to create three mini Mind Maps to help you to see the bigger picture. These can be drawn quite fast – but need to be as honest as possible.

Sketching mini Mind Maps in this way will help you to form a clearer idea of your personal views. This process is also useful whether you are studying a subject at school or college and are using Mind Maps to take notes and gather data, whether you are planning strategy in the workplace, organizing a social event, and many other applications.

Once you have looked at facts and feelings separately, you can combine them in a single Mind Map that will help you to see 'the big picture'.

Ask yourself what's happening:
- **What do you *think* about it?**

Place a single Key Word on each line to represent the different elements of your subject or situation.

- **What do you *feel* about it?**

Place a single Key Word on each line to represent your *feelings* about the subject or situation.

○ **What are *the facts* of the matter?**

Place a single Key Word on each line to represent *the facts*
surrounding the subject or situation. Ask yourself questions
such as:
*Why* is this?
*What* is the positive outcome?
*Who* is involved?
*Where* will it have an impact?
*How* can I achieve my goal?
If you're not sure of the accuracy of the facts, add a '?' to the
word.

These three mini Mind Maps will be an accurate reflection
of how you are thinking about and reacting to your situation at
this precise moment, and can be a very useful way of seeing 'the
wood *and* the trees' – especially if you are in a situation where
you know that your response may be extreme, irrational or
uncertain.

◉ What is guiding your decision-making at this point: the facts
or your feelings?

## Identify your choices

If you are unsure of your decision or viewpoint about a topic or situation, your next step should be to identify your choices in the matter.

Again, draw a picture of your main goal as your central image. Add at least two branches to represent your possible courses of action. These could be called 'Action' and 'No Action' (or any variations on this).

Without giving yourself too long to think (so that you ensure you are tapping into your para-conscious brain), sketch in your thoughts. Your results will help to remind you that some form of change is inevitable, and to decide what sort of outcome you would prefer.

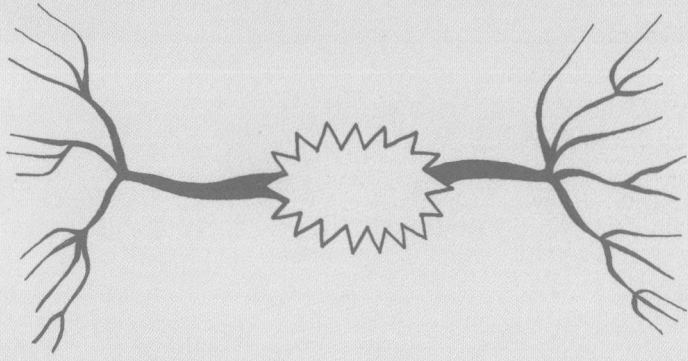

What is guiding your decision-making here? A strong opinion? A desire for change? A wish to escape the current situation? A hope that no action may be necessary after all?

This is quite a fast and powerful process and can reveal some interesting and unexpected thoughts, as well as give you a new perspective.

Once the mini brainstorms have helped you to see the core issues, you can combine your results in a larger, thematic Mind

Map that will help your brain to think more creatively about the future. You will start to make associations and see connections in the branches of the combined Mind Map that will drive you on much faster towards taking your ideal course of action.

## Taking stock

The more you look at your situation in detail, the better prepared and the more flexible you will be in tackling it.

In every so-called 'bad' situation there is always some 'good'; there is also likely to be some unknown territory that is neither 'good' nor 'bad' that represents a new opportunity, and will give you food for thought. I label this area 'fascinating'. The fascinating elements are those observations, questions, wonderings or imaginings that you can build on for the future. These can help you to decide your way forward.

First of all, imagine:

◉ If I did 'x' … what is the *worst* that could happen? When? Where?

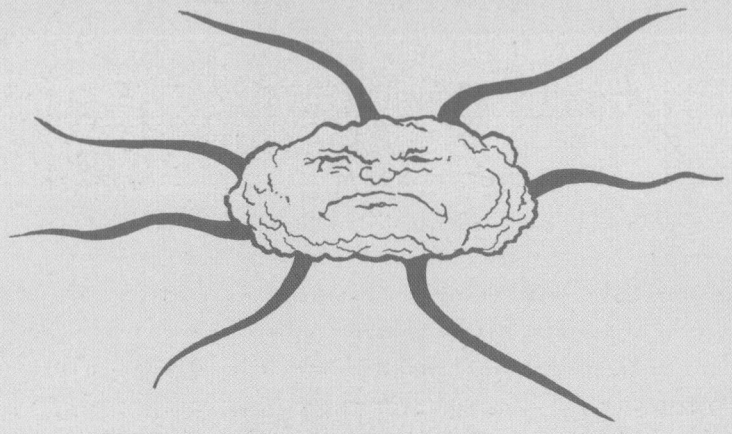

(Fill in the words on this mini Mind Map)

Then ask yourself:

○ If I did 'x' ... what would be the *good* in the situation?

(Fill in the words on this mini Mind Map)

The challenge is to get to a stage where you always manage to find the kernel of opportunity, or some aspect of the situation that represents something good for the future. Once you have found your positive focus you will be able to build on that, and create a new goal for yourself.

## Why taking a break is important

As those of you who have read my *Buzan Bites* book on *Memory* will know, the memory works best in 20–50–minute bursts, and remembers more information at the beginning or the end of a meeting, lesson or other encounter. Research shows that there is an initial *increase* in levels of understanding and recall after a short break. This is because the brain needs time to assimilate and understand information. (For a more detailed explanation of this phenomena and the reasons for it see *Use Your Head*, pages 62–9.) Conversely, the ability to recall information drops dramatically if we work for long periods *without* taking short breaks.

Bearing this in mind, if you have been focusing intently on something and are unclear as to how to tackle it, *take a break!* Listen to some music, go for a walk, talk to a friend. Do something that will stimulate your senses and allow your mind to assimilate the results of your work.

On your return, consider what has been useful in what you have done so far. Look at the information as though you were weighing up another person's situation. What do you see? What strikes you? Has your goal become clearer?

## The next step

The next step is to combine these elements into a complete Mind Map that has your personal goal at its centre. This is 'the Big Picture' that will help you to decide on your choices, opinions and what steps you need to take to achieve your goals.

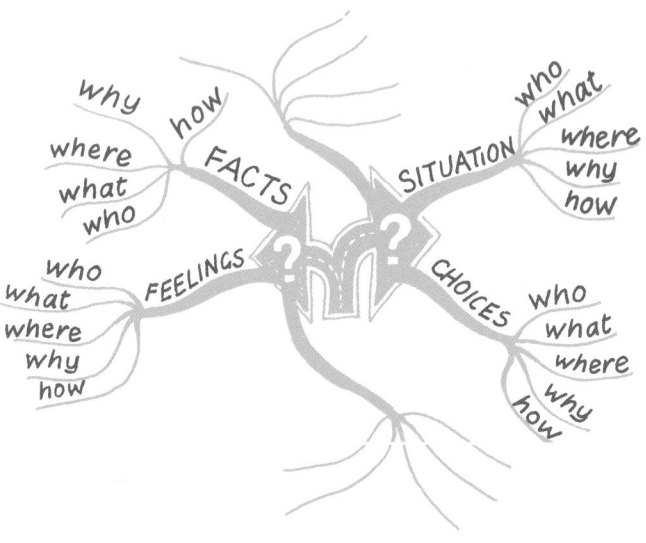

The following example was drawn by a female senior executive of a company who had decided it was time to take stock of her belief systems, her self and her direction for the future.

The more you practise these techniques, the more readily you will be able to use Mind Maps as a practical, everyday, working tool to keep your life in positive perspective and to help your decision-making.

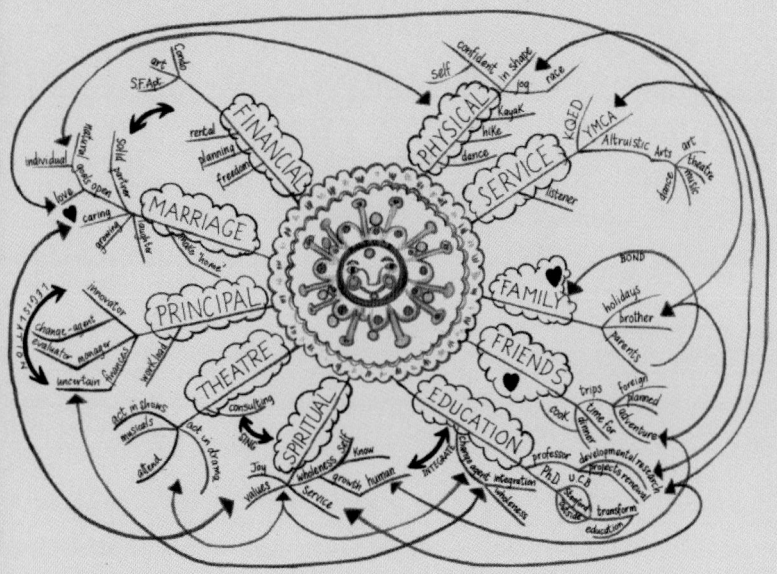

# 6 MIND MAPS FOR ALL OCCASIONS

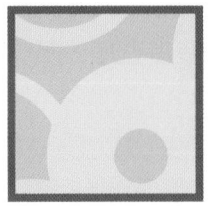

## Creating a Mind Map Diary

Traditional diaries are linear, time-bound and tied permanently to the days of the week and the months of the year. They are devices that aid planning and provide a retrospective record of what has taken place.

A Mind Map Diary, on the other hand, leads with your needs and desires as the main point of focus, while also incorporating the elements of a traditional diary.

The Mind Map Diary makes use of all the guidelines associated with creating a single Mind Map: colour, imagery, symbols, codes, humour, daydreams, wholeness, dimension, association and visual rhythm. It will give you a true reflection of what is going on in your mind, and is not just a time-management system, but a *life*-management system.

Your Mind Map Diary should ideally include the following stages.

## The Year Plan

At the beginning of each year – whether the year starts on 1 January, or some other preferred time (such as your birthday, or your business' end-of-year date) – create a Mind Map that sketches out your vision of the year ahead. It should be as positive as possible and should contain no specific details. (These will be taken account of in the monthly and daily plans that follow.) The Year Plan is a positive vision of your year ahead, and it should be an uplifting inspiration should challenges hit later in the year.

Your Year Plan should include:

⊙ Colours, codes, images.

⊙ You may also wish to include colour-coding that can be continued for consistency in your daily and monthly plans as the year progresses.

Your Year Plan could be organized by theme, by season, by month, or whatever basic ordering style you feel is appropriate.

Divisional branches will commonly include themes (Basic Ordering Ideas) such as:

- Family and friends
- Wealth and work
- Creativity and recreation
- Health and wellbeing.

## The Month Plan

Your monthly Mind Map Diary is a continuation and a development of your Year Plan, which takes each month of the year as its starting point. Your Mind Map Month Plan should include:

- Dates and days
- Hours of the day.

You may choose to use the Month Plan to plan ahead, or to review progress retrospectively. It can be a single, whole-month overview, or made of a combination of four weekly Mind Maps.

- Use of codes and colour-coding will give you an instant overview of what the month ahead has in store.
- As the year continues, lay each month's plan next to the other months, and your Year Plan, to help assess your priorities and progress for any period.
- Cross-referencing between months will make overall trends easier to spot.

## The Day Plan

A daily Mind Map is based on a 24-hour clock. In an ideal world you would create two Mind Maps for each day: one as a forward plan, and one as a retrospective stock-take of the day (which also forms the root of your plan for the following day).

Colour-coding and other symbols used in your Year Plan and your Month Plan can be applied consistently to your Day Plans, so that a quick browse over several days will give you an overview of 'the big picture' and help you decide on your point of focus for the days, weeks and months ahead.

## The benefits of a Mind Map Diary

There are many benefits of a Mind Map Diary. It is the only diary device that will give you both the big life picture and the details that make up that life, in one glance. You will be able to see, for example, when you had your last dental appointment as well as how you felt about life in general on the day in question; or you can identify the date on which you signed a contract for a major business deal, as well as how inspired you felt by a music event you attended that evening. A Mind Map Diary is not solely about facts and dates; it is also about sensation, feelings and inspirational moments.

A Mind Map Diary is:

⊙ A life-management tool that puts each life event in perspective.

⊙ An attractive visual reminder of your unique life.

⊙ A ready-reference for dates, trends and key events.

The Mind Map Diary system will put you firmly in control of your life and help you to prioritize those areas of your life that are most important to you. Regular use will help you to anticipate and solve problems, and to improve personal organization. If you have a family, you can adjust the system to encourage them to use Mind Maps on a regular basis too.

## Mind Maps at home

Whether or not you choose to use a Mind Map Diary on a regular basis, it can be extremely valuable to use an annual Mind Map to review past achievements and to take stock of your future goals. In no area of your life is this more important than in your personal and home life.

At school, college, and in business, planning tends to take place naturally, as part of the rhythm of the year and the flow of the season. In our rushed and frantic times it can often seem as if our home life has to be fitted in around duties and responsibilities at work and elsewhere.

Using Mind Maps to take regular stock of your life will ensure that your home–work balance is kept on track, and that you are where you want to be and are doing what you feel is the optimum with your life opportunity.

Importantly, Mind Maps can also be used in a constructive way as a method of exchanging ideas with friends and loved ones (see page 70).

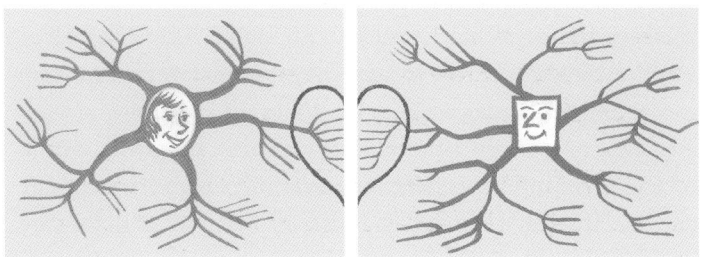

## Your whole life in a Mind Map

Take a few moments to create a Whole Life Mind Map. This needn't be complex. Put your SELF at the centre and include basic categories such as:

Home     Friends     Love     Family     Children
Work     Hobbies
Creativity     Finances     Health & Fitness
Spirit – or any others that suit your needs

Once you have completed the task – and you may want to tackle it in short brain-bursts over several days – take a good look at those areas of your talents that you might have allowed to lie fallow. Are there skills, interests, ambitions and priorities that you have overlooked recently? Assess and weigh up the results. Decide which of the ideas or themes has presented itself as your next goal.

Put this at the centre of a new Mind Map and this time add more proactive headings that encourage you to ask yourself: when you will act, how you will achieve, why you wish to, where you will be, who you need to help you achieve your goal and what you will be doing. (See page 53 for a reminder of how to do this.)

To maintain a healthy balance it is essential that, even during periods of time where the emphasis of your life changes, you keep the *overall* balance of your life stable. As one branch of your life grows, take care to keep the other basic branches strong too, so you do not neglect your roots and the sense of who you are. There are certain aspects of life that most of us will want to remain constant: the benefit of close family and/or friends, our personal interests, the challenge of work (whether or not we are paid for it).

Looking back at your annual Mind Maps will remind you of your journey and achievements to date. They are an ongoing record of a whole lifetime, and will give you (and possibly future generations) major insights into who you are and the path your life has taken – and is taking.

## Problem-solving with Mind Maps

Mind Maps are not just about an individual's view of the world; they can also be used to explore other people's views and as a way of resolving conflicts and problems. Mind Maps can be used as an objective method of comparing points of view, while giving all contributors an equal voice. They are, in the same moment, both a tool of practical and personal communication and a creative process of problem-solving and clarity.

### The way forward

If you are problem-solving with others, you may decide to create a joint Mind Map, or alternatively, each person might create separate Mind Maps, showing, for example:

Positives       Problems       Solutions

Each Mind Map should follow the now-familiar process of drawing a central image, followed by making a rapid-fire selection of associations and connections linked to the central theme. These are then organized under a selection of BOIs (see page 32) and sub-branches, and are eventually prioritized in the usual way.

## Sharing the results

If Mind Maps are being used to resolve a difficulty, it is important that you allow each other your say and that each of your views should be respected. For example, each of you could take it in turns to present your Mind Maps. Any negatives should be presented first, followed by positives and then solutions, so that discussion evolves in a positive fashion. There is then every chance that the solutions stage of the process will begin in a positive and hopeful frame of mind.

Even in moments of high feeling, there should be complete respect for each other's views. Each listener needs to remember that no matter how much they may disagree with what is being said, the presenter is saying something that *must be true from their personal perspective*.

An exchange of positive feedback will contribute positive energy and optimism to the discussion and lead all sides to listen more intently to each other's proposed solutions.

A discussion to find areas of mutual agreement can follow and a plan of action can be put in place that will agree time-bound points of action and follow-up. These solutions can be combined in a joint Mind Map.

**The overall benefits of this process include:**
- A fair exchange of ideas.
- A balanced view of the complete situation – including solutions.
- Honesty and respect between all participants.
- Any problems are put into perspective.
- The Mind Maps will stand as a record of the discussion.
- The process will achieve greater understanding.

The use of Mind Maps in personal and working relationships is potentially the most challenging, as well as the most rewarding, application of all the approaches described in the book. However, when approached with care and respect for one another, and for the relationship, the rewards are boundless.

The next chapters show how Mind Maps can be used to great effect in education, at work, and into the future.

# 7  MIND MAPS IN EDUCATION

One of the most exciting developments in my recent career has been the positive way in which educators and children around the world have begun to use Mind Maps as a teaching tool. Mind Maps can make teaching and learning a more stimulating, enjoyable and effective process.

Mind Maps are being used in degree courses for teacher training; for planning lessons; to explain complex concepts more  simply; for revision notes; as book summaries; and for homework. There are also a number of highly effective computer programs in use that make the creation and updating of Mind Maps very quick and easy. Those of you who would like to know more about computers and Mind Maps may like to refer to Chapter 28 of *The Mind Map® Book* (BBC Active).

The traditional 'norms' within education are that list-making and monochromatic note-making are good, whereas drawing pictures, doodling and daydreaming are innately wrong. As you will have gathered by now, my own beliefs and findings show that the opposite is true: traditional note-taking limits thought, whereas daydreaming and drawing will increase Radiant Thinking.

The younger a child is, the less he or she will have been conditioned by the limitations of traditional teaching beliefs, and the more naturally open they will be to the creative scope offered by Mind Mapping. Young children are natural Mind Mappers. They love to draw pictures, experiment with lettering, use emphasis, symbols, colour – not to mention stickers – when they are writing, drawing and communicating.

Explaining stories, science topics, history lessons, music rules or mathematical themes with the aid of Key Words and pictures in the form of a Mind Map will have a powerful and permanent impact on the ways in which a young child will take in, retain and recall information. Mind Map skills taught at an early age will become a skill that will be applied naturally throughout life.

For teachers and older students the applications are more practical: making teaching and learning an easier and more enjoyable experience. The following main applications outline the core benefits of Mind Mapping in education.

## Preparing lecture notes

Preparing a lecture in Mind Map form is much faster and more effective than writing out the lecture (or notes for the lecture) word by word and line by line. It has the advantage of giving the speaker an 'at a glance' overview of the whole topic.

Speaking from a Mind Map rather than from linear notes will also free up the lecturer to speak fluently from personal knowledge, rather than being tied to a rigid, leaden formula. Rather than focusing on a fear of losing his or her place in the notes, a Mind Map will encourage them to speak with passion from the heart of true knowledge. Every lecture will become slightly different – and more focused – as a result. The benefits to this approach to drafting and presenting a lecture are that students will remain engaged and interested, rather than drifting off to sleep because they feel they are being read to; and the lecturer will enjoy the experience of lecturing, rather than feeling stale with the boredom of repetition.

In the same way that the Mind Map Diary can be used to organize and plan a personal year, so too can a Mind Map be used to plan a whole year's study programme, the term ahead or even individual lessons and presentations.

## Preparing for exams

As an effective study aid, Mind Maps are in a league of their own, especially at exam time. If the true purpose of an exam is to test students' knowledge and understanding, Mind Maps are the perfect revision tool, as they allow students to encapsulate all they know – and all they need to know – into a single, visual reference. This means that basic facts can be seen and self-tested more quickly when revising; and students can measure personal progress by recreating Mind Maps from scratch and comparing the knowledge retained with the original 'master' Mind Map.

For all the reasons explained earlier (see Chapter 4), your memory will be attracted to remembering your Mind Map. This means that it is possible to store information in your mind in a precise way that is straightforward to recall, or to recreate when writing a test essay under exam conditions.

Many business, professional and teaching courses now incorporate Mind Maps into their training programmes and assess students on the quality of their Mind Maps in exams. They have been used with success by groups as diverse as the London Metropolitan Police and teachers of dyslexic children.

The key aspects in an effective teaching/ learning Mind Map are:

- ⊙ **Breadth of material covered.**
- ⊙ **Depth of material covered.**
- ⊙ **Own ideas included.**
- ⊙ **Learning-enhancing techniques included.**
  **e.g. colour, symbols, arrows.**

## The benefits of teaching and learning with Mind Maps

Mind Maps will automatically inspire the interest of students because they can be created as a cooperative exercise; this encourages students to be more receptive and attentive in class. Mind Maps also make lessons and presentations a spontaneous, creative and enjoyable experience for students and teacher alike. The flexibility of the Mind Map system allows the teacher to adapt and change lessons easily, according to the needs of the age group and the curriculum being taught. The method is especially useful for teaching those with learning disabilities, particularly dyslexia, because of the visual and creative focus.

Another advantage of the Mind Mapping system is that, unlike linear text, Mind Maps have the flexibility to show not just the facts, but also the *relationship between* those facts, which helps greater understanding. In addition, because they include relevant material only, students are unencumbered by endless bulky notes and more likely to be able to remember the important information for exams.

# 8 MIND MAPS IN YOUR PROFESSIONAL LIFE

This chapter looks at how Mind Maps can be used effectively for managing information in meetings; for planning and brainstorming; and when making presentations.

A Mind Map is the perfect tool for effective communication, management and project development at work. It is also the ideal device for productive brainstorming and can save hours in report writing. Mind Maps can be used to supercharge effective communication in:

**Meetings**      **Presentations**      **Management**

Many leaders of industry, politicians, educators and business people use Mind Maps to great effect within business management.

*For example:*
David Burt OBE, Chairman of Deutsch Ltd (an international company that produces high-quality connectors for the aeronautics industry) uses Mind Maps when communicating essential information to employees across his company. Alan Matcham of Oracle has used them for planning and prioritizing for over 20 years. He uses them in electronic form for sharing and developing ideas with colleagues worldwide.

## Making the most of meetings
Every person who attends a meeting will have something to contribute – either within the meeting itself, or as a result of information learned in the meeting.

## Guidelines for using a Mind Map to take notes in a meeting:

⊙ The central image will be the main subject of the meeting.

⊙ The Basic Ordering Ideas (BOIs) that form the core branches of the Mind Map will be the main items that are on the agenda.

⊙ As the meeting progresses, new ideas and thoughts can be added as sub-branches to the BOIs.

⊙ If the meeting is made up of a series of presentations you may also want to create mini Mind Maps to represent the ideas presented by each of the speakers.

⊙ As long as all versions are on the same sheet of paper it will be quite easy to indicate cross-references and themes as they begin to emerge.

## Guidelines for Mind Mapping as a group

In a group situation, it is useful to have a Mind Map that is on general show to keep track of shared ideas as well as encouraging people to create their own individual Mind Maps. In this way no contribution will be overlooked, and ideas can be added later.

Effective use of colour coding, symbols, arrows and other devices will ensure that all elements of the Mind Map are drawn together at the end of the meeting. Since everyone in the group has had some input, there will be a sense of shared ownership when the final version is circulated to all attendees.

In traditional brainstorming situations there is an ongoing danger that good ideas are not voiced, or that others become superseded as the meeting progresses by the latest or loudest voice. Traditional methods of meeting-structure and minute-taking increasingly restrict the flexibility of communication as a meeting progresses: a Mind Map has the opposite effect allowing the categorization and growth of ideas that may occur at *any stage* of that meeting.

A group Mind Map incorporates two elements of the meeting:

**Brainstorming**      **Planning**

Since a Mind Map has the advantage of giving a clear and balanced view of the true content of the meeting, they are especially valuable when chairing or minuting meetings. The Mind Map framework will be based around the items on the agenda. Thoughts, discussion points raised, and points of action can be added to each of the branches and annotated with the initials of each contributor. This approach gives more credence and balance to each of the topics raised (coding can be used to weight the importance of each contribution if necessary).

**The core benefits of Mind Maps for meetings are:**

⊙ They ensure everyone understands each other's viewpoint.

⊙ All contributions are placed fairly in context.

⊙ All individual contributions are included, which increases the energy, enthusiasm and cooperation of members of the group.

⊙ Each member of the meeting has a complete record of the meeting, which ensures that everyone understands and remembers key decisions taken.

⊙ Efficient Mind Mapping can speed up meetings and the time it takes to make decisions.

⊙ Mind Maps increase the probability of goals being achieved.

# Communicating and presenting information

## Effective communication

Effective communication is an absolute essential in business. If communication is weak or founders departments falter, divisions lose their way and businesses fail.

There are several reasons why Mind Maps are ideally suited to business management. People in business are working in an environment where time is of the essence, and Mind Maps allow complex and detailed information to be communicated quickly, simply and in a way that everyone will understand.

The needs of business are similar to those in education, in that people need to be kept motivated and also engaged with what is going on. A Mind Map can be understood by everyone; it can be kept updated and circulated easily; total involvement will result in greater commitment from all staff.

## Powerful presentations

A powerful presentation will enthuse and engage an audience, making it the ideal way of communicating essential information to a large number of people. The benefits are similar to those outlined on page 75, for lecturers. A poor presentation, on the other hand, will have the opposite and negative effect; hence the prospect of being asked to make a presentation fills many people with fear and dread.

Preparation and planning are the main keys to making a successful presentation, and a Mind Map is the perfect tool to help you achieve your aim.

The guidelines for preparation are very similar to those laid out for teaching and self-assessment:

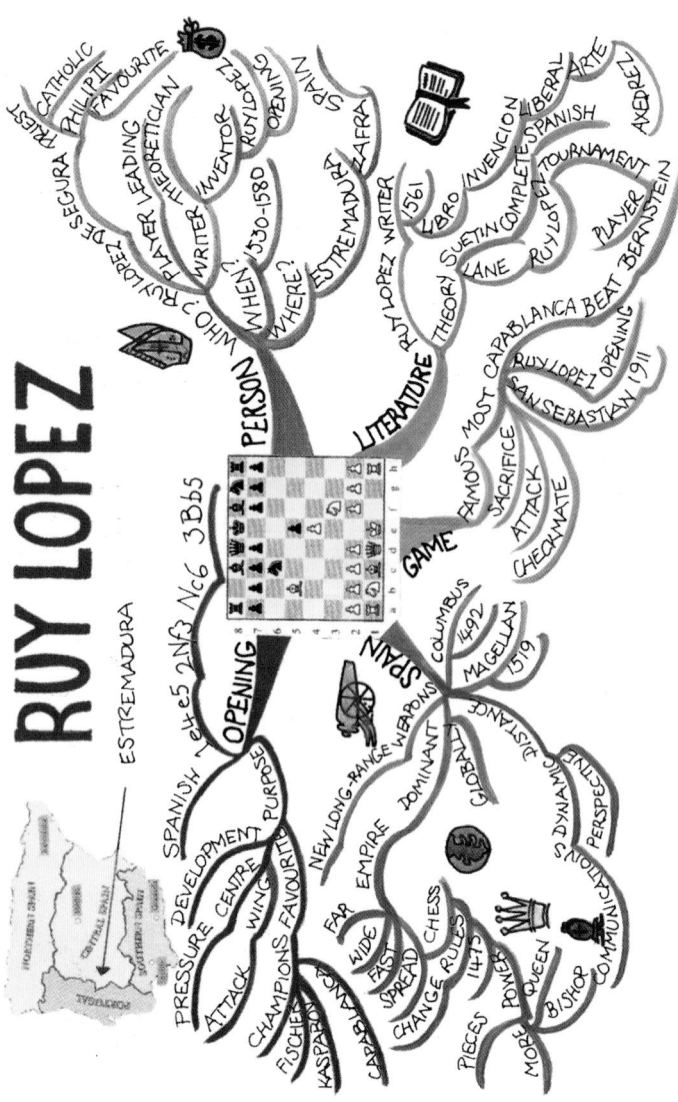

**A Mind Map prepared by Raymond Keen, OBE, Grandmaster in Chess, in preparation for a lecture given on Spanish television.**

⊙ Select a core, central image to represent the main theme of your talk.

⊙ Mind Map a quick-fire burst of ideas that immediately come to mind in relation to your main topic.

⊙ Select the strongest topics to become the main branches of your Mind Map and challenge the ideas to see whether any other topics come to mind that should be included.

⊙ Focus on each topic on each branch of your Mind Map and think of a maximum of 50 Key Words and Images combined that can be related to the core topics. You will be aiming to speak for approximately one minute for each Key Word.

Next decide on the order of priority for each topic: pare down the topics in each section to the essentials, and number each branch so that you are in no doubt as to the order of the material to be presented.

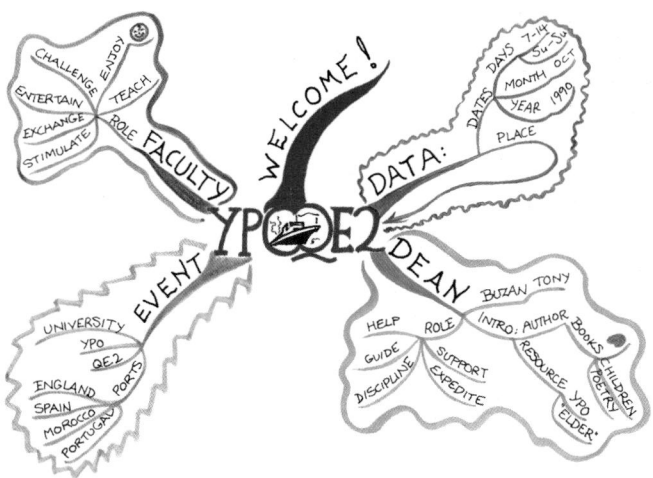

**A Mind Map prepared by Tony Buzan, when Dean of the Young Presidents' Organization Faculty, for his welcoming speech to an international body of professors and dignitaries.**

⊙ Add codes, colours, arrows and other links to indicate connections, associations and practical interventions – such as slides to be used, videos or other materials to be introduced, and so on.

⊙ Add times to each topic – then all you need to do is follow your own instructions!

There are many advantages to using Mind Maps for speech preparation, similar to those experienced by teachers.

⊙ You will keep your audience interested because the presentation will be lively and original.

⊙ You will be free of detailed notes, and more able to be yourself and to reinforce speech with physical gestures.

⊙ Your talk will be the perfect balance between a structured pre-planned talk and a spontaneous chat – without the rustle of pages or the rigidity of a PowerPoint presentation.

⊙ You will be free to involve members of your audience and to take questions from the floor, if appropriate.

⊙ You will find it easier to update and adapt the talk as appropriate for your audience and the time and occasion.

A Mind Map gives a presenter the freedom and flexibility to speak naturally *and* in a well-ordered fashion. If you are interrupted part way through, the Mind Map format will allow the flexibility to incorporate diversions or questions into the whole. You can also speed up, or slow down your presentation with ease if need be.

> **In a nutshell, the benefits of using Mind Maps for presentations are:**
> - They increase your involvement and eye contact with the audience.
> - You will be free to be yourself and to keep on the move – which will engage people's interest.
> - Both the speaker and the listener will be more involved with the presentation.
> - Mind Maps allow you greater flexibility and adaptability – enabling you to expand or contract points as required.
> - The resulting talk is likely to be more memorable, effective and enjoyable than a presentation given from written notes.
> - You will never repeat the same performance.

## Mind Maps for managers

Each and every one of us is a manager. We all manage our time, our life, the way we communicate with friends, colleagues, and our plans for the future. The plans that we commit to paper are more likely to become reality than those we retain in our head because we have given them vision and substance. You will already know that the most effective format for expressing those ideas on paper is in Mind Map form.

Mind Maps can be used by every individual in business in any situation where linear notes would normally be taken; examples of these situations include:
- Managing structures and change
- Research and development/future priorities

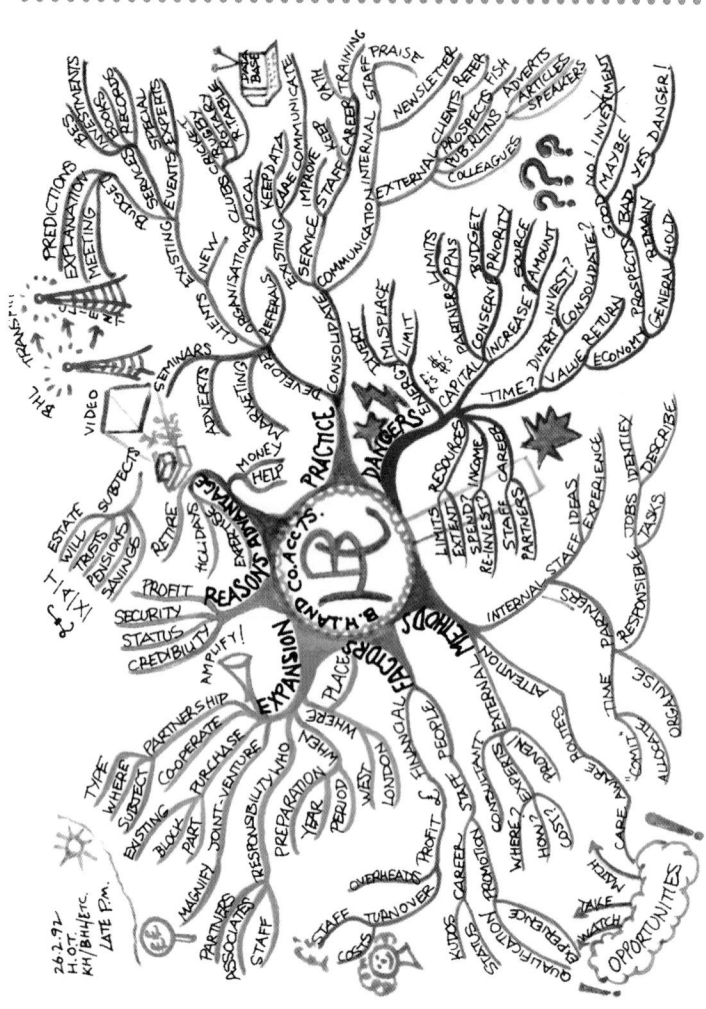

**A Mind Map prepared by Brian Lee of B.H. Lee & Company, Accountants, on the developments, dangers and expansion of a business practice.**

- Sales and marketing strategy
- Leadership skills, training and staff development
- Time-management systems
- Profitability and viability
- Future vision/expansion.

# 9 MIND MAPS FOR THE FUTURE

You have just shifted your thinking by centuries!

During the industrial revolution, standardized linear note taking was a reflection of the rigidity and linearization necessary in factories, production lines and the developing military. Thinking was also of the simple 'either-or' variety.

Such thinking and such linear methodologies are not relevant for an age exploding with information and knowledge, and requiring thinking of a non-linear, Radiant, far more rapid and flexible nature. You have just learned the tool that reflects this.

**Mind Mapping is to the Twenty-first Century, what linear note taking was to the Nineteenth Century.**

Once you are used to creating Mind Maps you will find that you start to use them intuitively to make notes, 'lists', plans and to communicate ideas, until they become an invaluable and indispensable part of your life.

Remember, as you develop your Mind Mapping skills, that you have two universes of stars in your brain. The first are your brain cells, the *million million* super mini-computers that are shaped like stars radiating light.

The second is the infinite universe populated by the stars of your thought: the centres of your ideas that radiate associations and that connect with each other in limitless networks.

It is these two universes that form the basis for, and are reflected by, your Mind Maps. When you Mind Map, you are tapping into the power of not one, but *two* universes.

Mind Maps solve the age old dilemma of not being able to see the wood for the trees or the trees because of the wood. With a Mind Map you can *simultaneously* see both the wood *and* the trees.

And while on that theme, a senior Civil Servant noticed, after months of using Mind Maps, that the volume of his notes had significantly decreased, while the power and precision of them had significantly increased. As a concerned environmentalist he coined the phrase: '*Use a Mind Map, save a tree!*'

Mind Maps give you control of, and guidance for, both your thoughts and your emotions.

**Mind Maps are a thinking and a feeling tool.**

As you will increasingly see, Mind Maps have as many applications as there are possibilities for the use of thought – infinite.

By continuing to use them and study more about their theory and application, you will grow into a true Twenty-first Century thinker with a rapidly developing and expanding 'Brain Bank Account' of Intellectual Capital.

In the Matter of your Mind, you will find that your Mind *does* Matter, and that Mind Maps are a wonderful way to use, nurture and develop it.

# Further reading

For those who are ready to take their knowledge to a deeper level, my Mind Set series contains in-depth guidance on how to make maximum use of your mind and your memory. The following books are available from BBC Active:

Use Your Head
The Mind Map® Book
The Illustrated Mind Map® Book
The Speed Reading Book
Use Your Memory
Master Your Memory